# LEWIS AND CLARK

## Explorers of the American West

by Steven Kroll

illustrated by Richard Williams

Holiday House/New York

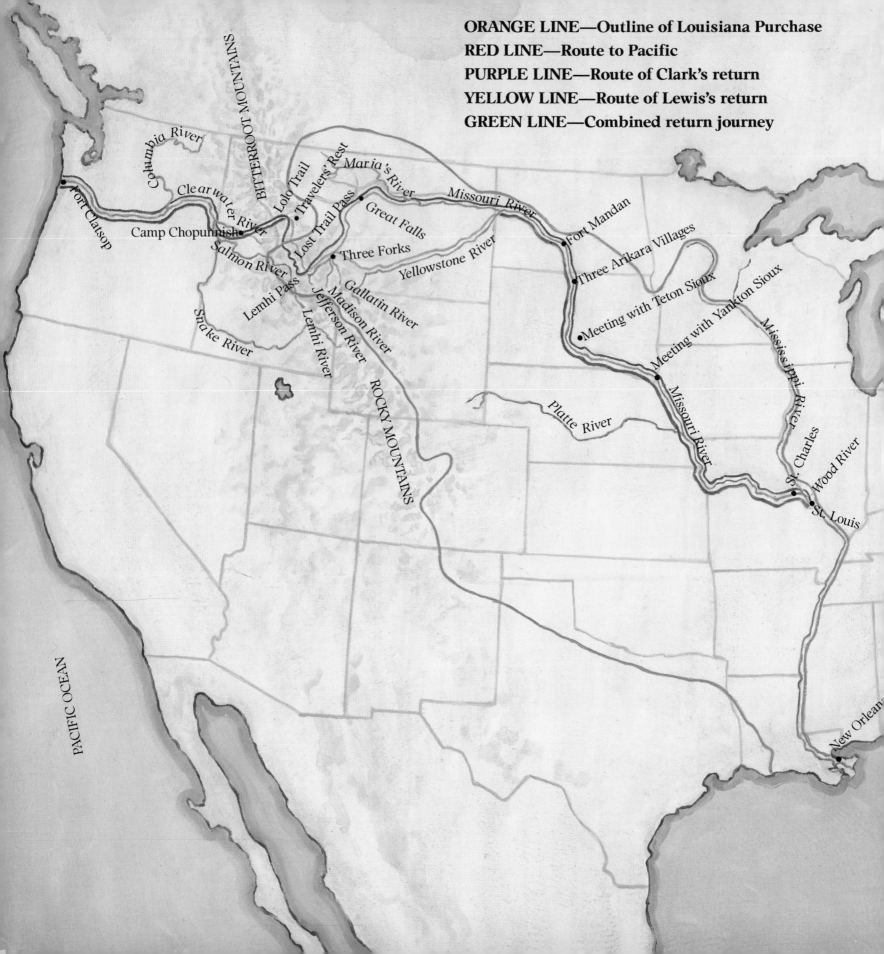

ORANGE LINE—Outline of Louisiana Purchase
RED LINE—Route to Pacific
PURPLE LINE—Route of Clark's return
YELLOW LINE—Route of Lewis's return
GREEN LINE—Combined return journey

# THE LOUISIANA PURCHASE

In 1803, the United States was just twenty years old. There were seventeen states in the Union, and American territory reached only as far west as the Mississippi River.

On the other side of the Mississippi, between the river and the Rocky Mountains, was the unexplored Louisiana Territory. In 1800 Napoleon Bonaparte, emperor of France, had taken Louisiana back from Spain, who had ruled it since 1763.

President Thomas Jefferson did not want the French army threatening America's western border. He wasn't ready to risk the closing of the port of New Orleans, at the mouth of the Mississippi and vital to American trade. In March 1803, Jefferson instructed his minister to France, Robert R. Livingston, to buy New Orleans from Napoleon.

Napoleon had been unable to put down a slave rebellion in Haiti, led by the great black general, Toussaint L'Ouverture. Soon he would be fighting another war with Great Britain. Involved in too many places at once, he decided to get out of North America. He offered to sell the whole of the Louisiana Territory for sixty million francs (about fifteen million dollars).

Jefferson felt this new land should be explored. Even before the United States took possession of the territory late in 1803 and early in 1804, the president had been discussing an expedition to the Pacific Ocean.

On June 20, 1803, President Thomas Jefferson asked his private secretary, Captain Meriwether Lewis, to lead an expedition from the Mississippi River to the West Coast.

Meriwether Lewis

William Clark

Lewis agreed. As co-leader, he chose William Clark, who had once been his commanding officer in the army. On their journey, they would explore ways of opening the fur trade. They would try to find a water route across the continent that would make travel easier. They would also study the land and animals and learn more about the Indians in the West.

The expedition was called the Corps of Discovery. Between December 1803 and May 1804, it took shape at the mouth of the Wood River, where the Missouri and Mississippi rivers meet. Clark trained the men while Lewis spent much of his time in St. Louis, making preparations.

York

A typical riverman

Seaman

In the party were fourteen soldiers; nine volunteers from Kentucky; Clark's slave, York; two French rivermen; an interpreter; and Lewis's Newfoundland dog, Seaman. There were also nine rivermen and seven soldiers who went along for extra protection in the wilderness. These extra men planned to return home that fall.

On a rainy Monday, May 14, 1804, Clark and the men started up the Missouri. Lewis was in St. Louis and would join the expedition in a few days.

The group traveled in a fifty-five-foot keelboat and in two huge dugout canoes called pirogues. They led two horses along the bank to bring in game shot by the hunters.

The boats carried clothing, tools, scientific books, medicine, rifles, goods for trading with the Indians, and a special, powerful air gun to impress them. In case they had no other transportation, Lewis had included a collapsible iron canoe he called *The Experiment*. In the event they ran out of food, he had brought a thick, gooey "portable soup."

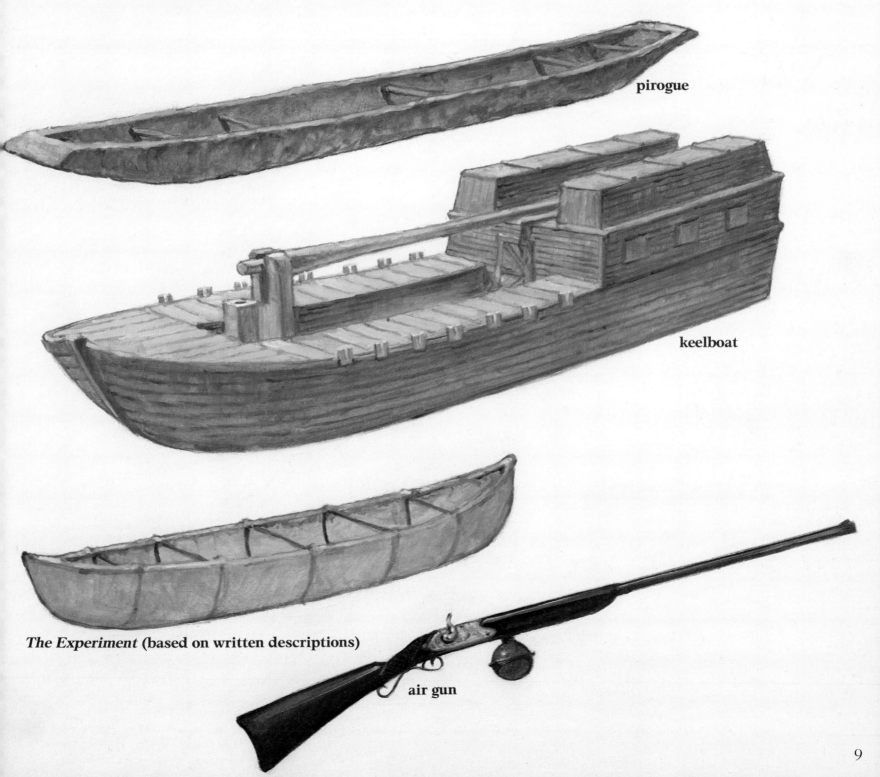

pirogue

keelboat

*The Experiment* (based on written descriptions)

air gun

9

After two days, the Corps of Discovery reached St. Charles. Five days later Lewis joined them, and their journey began. The swift current and sandbars of the Missouri made rowing hard and poling tricky. Often the men had to tow the boats through the muddy water.

Lewis frequently walked onshore, taking notes on plants and animals. Clark stayed with the boats, mapping their course.

It got very hot. Mosquitoes, gnats, and ticks tormented everyone. Some of the men got sick. But the hunters kept the group well stocked with game, and on July 21, they reached the mouth of the Platte River.

High on a bluff three days later, they met with Oto and Missouri Indians. Lewis and Clark couldn't understand the Indian language. Their interpreter, George Drouillard, translated the Indian sign language. Lewis gave a speech about peace and trade with Americans. He told them that the "Great Father" in Washington wanted the chiefs to visit. Then he draped medals from President Jefferson around the chiefs' necks. He fired the air gun, hoping the noise would awe them.

Soon after, Sergeant Charles Floyd died of a burst appendix. He was the only member of the expedition to die during the two years, four months, and nine days of the journey.

Pressing on, the men began to see animals they had never even imagined: antelope and prairie dogs, a white pelican, a jackrabbit, coyotes. As trees became fewer, buffalo herds seemed to blanket the plains.

On August 29, the Corps met with a friendly tribe of Yankton Sioux. A few weeks later, they discovered that their cousins upriver, the Teton Sioux, were not so friendly. The Corps spent four tense days with them before meeting the more hospitable Arikaras, who were farmers. They admired Clark's slave, York, the first black man they had ever seen.

14

Toward the end of October, the expedition stopped for the winter near the villages of the Mandan and Hidatsa Indians. The men completed Fort Mandan on November 20. The fort had eight connected log cabins arranged in a *V* with a high fence at the open end.

**Hidatsa**　　　　　　**Teton Sioux**　　　　　　**Mandan**　　　　　　**Yankton Sioux**

15

Snow, ice, and below zero temperatures made everyone miserable, but riverman Pierre Cruzatte lifted everyone's spirits by playing his fiddle as the group danced at Christmas. The Mandans and Hidatsas welcomed the explorers to their large, round lodges. The Hidatsa chiefs told Lewis and Clark what they knew about the geography of the Rocky Mountains.

16

During the winter, Toussaint Charbonneau, a French Canadian living with the Hidatsas, joined the expedition as an interpreter. His teenaged Shoshone wife, Sacagawea, joined, too. On February 11, Sacagawea gave birth to a son, Jean Baptiste.

On April 7, 1805, Lewis and Clark sent several soldiers and rivermen back to St. Louis on the keelboat. They were to take four magpies and a prairie dog, boxes of skins and horns, Indian articles, small samples of soil and plants, and Clark's maps and charts to President Jefferson.

That same day, the Corps of Discovery, now numbering thirty-two and a baby, pushed on upriver into the unknown. They traveled in the two pirogues and in six dugout canoes they had made during the winter.

It stayed cold, but the plains were green and game was everywhere. The Corps began to encounter grizzly bears.

Lewis first saw the Rocky Mountains on May 26. He wrote in his journal of his joy but also of "the difficulties which this snowey barrier would most probably throw in my way to the Pacific . . ." Already he seemed aware that no river could come close to crossing these mountains, that there would be no water route to the West Coast.

19

On June second the expedition came to a fork in the river. Which branch was the Missouri? If the explorers made a wrong choice, the passes through the Rockies might be blocked off by snow before they could reach them.

The north fork was muddy like the Missouri, the south fork clear and gravelly, as if it came from the mountains. Only the captains preferred the second choice.

Lewis went ahead on land to explore the south fork. When he reached the Great Falls of the Missouri River on June 13, he knew he and Clark had made the right choice.

The falls were magnificent, but there were so many it took a month to get around them. With bleeding feet, the men made makeshift wagons and cleared eighteen miles of undergrowth. There were hailstorms, mosquitoes, rattlesnakes, and grizzlies. When they finally struggled back to the Missouri River, *The Experiment's* buffalo-hide cover leaked, and it was left behind.

On July 19, the Corps passed through a huge chasm Lewis named the
Gates of the Rocky Mountains. When they reached the Three Forks of the
Missouri, Sacagawea declared that the Hidatsas had kidnapped her from
the Shoshones at this very spot.

Lewis and Clark named the three forks the Jefferson, Madison, and
Gallatin rivers. They took the westernmost one, the Jefferson. When they
turned up a stream into the mountains, they began to realize they would
need horses to continue.

From Sacagawea, the Corps knew they were in Shoshone territory. When they found a tribe from which they hoped to get horses, the chief, Cameahwait, turned out to be Sacagawea's brother!

Sacagawea helped interpret. The Corps traded goods for horses, hid their canoes by sinking them with stones, and set out over Lemhi Pass to the Lemhi Fork of the Salmon River.

A week later, through snow and sleet, they struggled over Lost Trail Pass into Flathead Valley and a camp they called Travelers' Rest. Then they followed the Lolo Trail across the Bitterroot Mountains. Wet, cold, and hungry, they could find no game. When Lewis's "portable soup" became unbearable, they killed and ate a colt.

23

Reaching the Clearwater River, the Corps met a tribe of friendly Nez Percé, or "pierced nose," Indians. Chief Twisted Hair agreed to look after their horses until their return. On October 7th, they started down the Clearwater to the Snake and Columbia rivers in five dugout canoes they had made during their visit.

Sometimes the men lowered the canoes through the rapids on ropes. Other times they ran the rapids or carried everything around them. When they glimpsed an Indian in a sailor's jacket, they knew their goal was near. They reached the Pacific Ocean in mid-November.

It rained all winter. The men built Fort Clatsop inland from the sea. Lewis and Clark worked on their notes and journals. Everyone was bored and ill. On March 23, 1806, they started for home. If they didn't reach the Missouri before it froze, they'd be spending another winter in the wilderness.

Traveling upstream, the Corps had to lug the canoes around the larger rapids and tow them up the smaller ones. They visited Chief Yelleppet and the friendly Walla Walla Indians. Then they moved out overland and set up Camp Chopunnish fifty or sixty miles above the mouth of the Clearwater. Some of the men traded buttons from their uniforms to the Nez Percé for food. Clark traded medical advice and medicines.

Chief Twisted Hair returned most of their horses, and on June 15, they started back over the Lolo Trail. Forced to turn around because the snow was so deep, they set out again on June 24 with three Nez Percé guides. Six days of struggle brought them to Travelers' Rest.

There the expedition separated. With most of the group, Clark traveled south, then east to explore the Yellowstone River. With a few men, Lewis traveled east to Great Falls, then north to explore Maria's River. On July 27, Blackfeet Indians tried to steal the rifles belonging to Lewis's party. Two of the Indians were killed.

Lewis and Clark caught up with one another on the Missouri on August 12. Before that, Pierre Cruzatte accidentally shot Lewis in the upper thigh while they were hunting.

Going downstream on the Missouri was much easier than coming up. The Corps left Charbonneau, Sacagawea, and the baby, whom Clark had

called "Pomp," with the Mandans on August 17. The Mandan chief Big White agreed to go along to Washington.

The Corps reached St. Louis on September 23, 1806. People lined up along the riverbank and cheered. The entire nation had thought the members of the expedition had died in the wilderness. Only President Jefferson had held out hope that Lewis and Clark would return.

# AFTERWORD

Lewis and Clark gathered information on 178 new kinds of plants, 122 new kinds of animals, and more than 40 Indian tribes. Because of their expedition, trappers and later, settlers moved out over what would soon be a nation stretching from coast to coast.

Early in 1807, Meriwether Lewis became governor of the Louisiana Territory. He moved to St. Louis but was never happy in his job. When the War and Treasury departments questioned his official expenses, he started for Washington on September 4, 1809, to defend himself. On October 11, traveling through Tennessee, he was found shot to death at Grinder's Stand on the Natchez Trace, a narrow wilderness road. It remains unclear whether Lewis killed himself or was murdered.

When Lewis became governor, William Clark was appointed brigadier general of the Louisiana Militia. He married on January 5, 1808, moved to St. Louis, and had five children. In 1813 he was appointed governor of what was now the Missouri Territory, as well as superintendent of Indian Affairs. Governor until Missouri became a state in 1820, he continued to help the Indians afterward. He died in St. Louis in 1838.

Before leaving the expedition, Charbonneau and Sacagawea had promised to take Jean Baptiste to Clark when he was old enough to leave his mother. In 1810 they arrived in St. Louis, and Clark arranged for the boy's education. Charbonneau returned to live with the Indians. Sacagawea probably died of "putrid" fever in 1812, but some still believe she lived on until 1884 and died with her own people, the Shoshones, in the far West.

York did not return to St. Louis with Clark. His wife belonged to a family near Louisville, Kentucky, and Clark agreed to hire him out in the area so he could be close to her. Eventually, Clark freed York and set him up in a carting business between Nashville and Richmond. The former slave later died of cholera, although some say he journeyed back to the Crow Indians and became a chief.

# IMPORTANT DATES

| | |
|---|---|
| May 14, 1804 | The expedition begins. The Corps of Discovery starts up the Missouri River. |
| September 25–29 | Meeting with the Teton Sioux. |
| November 20 | Fort Mandan completed for the winter. |
| April 7, 1805 | With animals and other specimens, the keelboat leaves for St. Louis. The same day, the Corps of Discovery starts up-river into the unknown. |
| May 26 | Lewis first sees the Rocky Mountains. |
| June 13 | The expedition reaches the Great Falls of the Missouri River. |
| August 12 | Lewis crosses the Continental Divide, where eastern rivers flow east and western rivers flow west. |
| September 9 | Having crossed Lost Trail Pass, the expedition camps at Travelers' Rest. |
| October 16 | The expedition reaches the Columbia River. |
| Mid-November | The expedition reaches the Pacific Ocean. |
| December 31 | Fort Clatsop completed. |
| March 23, 1806 | The Corps of Discovery starts home. |
| May 14 | The expedition sets up Camp Chopunnish above the mouth of the Clearwater River. |
| June 24 | Forced back from the Lolo Trail, the expedition sets out again and reaches Travelers' Rest in six days. |
| July 3 | The expedition splits up, Lewis to explore Maria's River and Clark the Yellowstone. |
| August 12 | The expedition is reunited. |
| September 23 | The Corps of Discovery reaches St. Louis. |

---

*To the Blechers:* George, Lone, Lilly-Marie, and Haldan/S.K.

To my wife, Malgorzata, and my daughter, Dominique/R.W.

Text copyright © 1994 by Steven Kroll. Illustrations copyright © 1994 by Richard Williams. All rights reserved.
Printed in the United States of America.
Library of Congress Cataloging-in-Publication Data. Kroll, Steven. Lewis and Clark : explorers of the American West / by Steven Kroll ;
illustrated by Richard Williams.    p.    cm.
Summary: Introduces Meriwether Lewis and William Clark and their expedition of 1804–6 through the Louisiana Territory, opening
the land from the Mississippi River to the Pacific Ocean.
ISBN 0-8234-1034-X
1. Lewis and Clark Expedition (1804–1806)—Juvenile literature. 2. Lewis, Meriwether, 1774–1809—Juvenile literature.
3. Clark, William, 1770–1838—Juvenile literature.  [1. Lewis and Clark Expedition (1804–1806)   2. Lewis, Meriwether, 1774–1809.
3. Clark, William, 1770–1838.   4. Explorers.]   I. Williams, Richard, 1950– ill.   II. Title.
F592.7.K76   1994    92-40427    CIP    AC    917804'2—dc20
ISBN 0-8234-1273-3 (pbk.)

# INDEX